the ☾ of Hope

Those who **hope** *in the* **LORD**
will renew their strength.

Isaiah 40:31 NIV

To _____

_____

_____

_____

From _____

Date _____

Our Daily Bread
Publishing™

the **Gift** *of* **Hope**

© 2022 Our Daily Bread Publishing

the **Gift** concept

Developed and designed by 2K/DENMARK

Typeset using the Triptych font family

ISBN 978-1-64070-192-2

Printed in China

Hope. People often use the word lightly. I **hope** it doesn't rain, they might say. With the power of a wish, but without any real conviction that there is better than a fifty-fifty chance of what they hope for.

Or maybe they speak more seriously: **Hopefully** you'll get that raise. With the strength of desire that, if realized, will be considered beneficial. They feel pretty good about the potential.

Only rarely do people embrace hope with confidence: I have **hope** that I'm prepared to face what tomorrow brings. With an absolute expectation, a total trust that what they believe will come to pass. The strange thing about that kind of anticipation is that when tomorrow comes, even if it brings along the entirely unexpected, their confidence doesn't seem to waver. And in an almost absurd way, their hope is fact.

That's the kind of hope that the Bible talks about. **Hope** that's already a truth. Living and eternal **hope.** Wouldn't we all like that! Wander in these words from God's book. Take them in all at once, or sit with just one page at a time. And find strength and comfort in the message of **hope** found here.

For I know the plans and thoughts that I have for you," says the **LORD**, "plans for peace and well-being and not for disaster, to give you a future and a **hope**."

Jeremiah 29:11 AMP

Those who **hope**
in the **LORD**
will renew
their strength;
they will fly up
on wings like eagles;
they will run
and not be tired,
they will walk
and not be weary.

Isaiah 40:31 CEB

The **LORD**
is a shelter
for the oppressed,
a refuge in times
of trouble.
Those who know
your name trust in **you,**
for you, O **LORD,**
do not abandon those
who search for **you.**

Psalm 9:9–10 NLT

LORD, ...
You listen to the
longings
of those who suffer.
You offer them **hope**,
and **you** pay attention
to their cries for help.

Psalm 10:16–17 CEV

For **God**
so loved the world
that **he** gave
his one and only **Son**,
that whoever believes
in **him** shall not perish
but have eternal life.

For **God** did not send **his Son** into the world to condemn the world, but to save the world through **him**.

John 3:16–17 NIV

In **Christin** we can come before **God** with freedom and without fear.

Ephesians 3:12 NCV

Let us then
approach
God's throne
of grace
with **confidence**,
so that we
may receive mercy
and find grace
to help us
in our time
of need.

Hebrews 4:16 NIV

He gives strength
to the weary
and increases
the power of the weak.

Isaiah 40:29 NIV

Jesus:

"Come to **me**,
all you that are weary
and are carrying
heavy burdens,
and **I** will give you rest.

Take **my** yoke upon you,
and learn from **me**;
for **I** am gentle
and humble in heart,
and you will find rest
for your souls."

Matthew 11:28–29 NRSV

Jesus:
"**My** sheep recognize
my voice. **I** know them,
and they follow **me**.
I give them real
and eternal life.
They are protected
from the Destroyer
for good.

No one can steal them
from out of **my** hand.
The **Father** who put them
under **my** care
is so much greater
than the Destroyer
and Thief.
No one could ever
get them away
from **him**."

John 10:27–29 MSG

God will take care of all your needs with the wonderful blessings that come from **Christ Jesus!**

Philippians 4:19 CEV

You parents
—if your children
ask for a loaf of bread,
do you give them
a stone instead?
Or if they ask for a fish,
do you give them a snake?
Of course not!

So if you sinful people
know how to
give good gifts
to your children,
how much more
will your **heavenly Father**
give good gifts
to those who ask **him.**

Matthew 7:9–11 NLT

And we know that **God** causes everything to work together for the good of those who love **God** and are called according to **his** purpose for them.

Romans 8:28 NLT

We put our **hope** in the **LORD**. **He** is our help and our shield.

Psalm 33:20 CEB

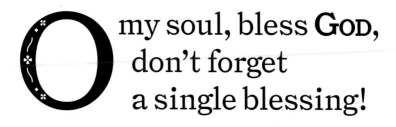

O my soul, bless **GOD**,
　　don't forget
　　a single blessing!

He forgives your sins
　　—every one.
He heals your diseases
　　—every one.
He redeems you from hell
　　—saves your life!

He crowns you
    with love and mercy
    —a paradise crown.
He wraps you in
    goodness
    —beauty eternal.
He renews your youth
    —you're always young
    in **his** presence.

Psalm 103:2–5 MSG

For whatever was written in earlier times was written for our instruction, so that through endurance and the encouragement of the Scriptures we might have **hope** and overflow with **confidence** in **His** promises.

Romans 15:4 AMP

Do the skies themselves send down showers? No, it is **you**, LORD our **God**. Therefore our **hope** is in you, for **you** are the one who does all this.

Jeremiah 14:22 NIV

With eager **hope**, the creation looks forward to the day when it will join **God's** children in glorious freedom from death and decay.

Romans 8:20–21 NLT

We, too,
wait with
eager **hope**
for the day
when **God** will give us
our full rights as
his adopted children,
including the new bodies
he has promised us.
We were given this **hope**
when we were saved.

Romans 8:23–24 NLT

Understand the **hope** that was given to you when **God** chose you. Then you will discover the glorious blessings that will be yours together with all of **God's** people.

Ephesians 1:18 CEV

What a **God** we have! And how fortunate we are to have **him**, this **Father** of our **Master Jesus**! Because **Jesus** was raised from the dead, we've been given a brand-new life and have everything to live for,

including a future
in heaven
—and the future
starts now!
God is keeping
careful watch over us
and the future.
The Day is coming
when you'll have it all
—life healed and whole.

1 Peter 1:3–5 MSG

We fix our eyes
not on what
is seen,
but on what is unseen,
since what is seen
is temporary,
but what is unseen
is eternal.

2 Corinthians 4:18 NIV

Let your **hope** make you glad. Be patient in time of trouble and never stop praying.

Romans 12:12 CEV

This is
the **confidence**
we have
in approaching **God**:
that if we ask
anything according to
his will, **he** hears us.

1 John 5:14 NIV

L

et us seize
and hold tightly
the confession
of our **hope**
without wavering,
for **He** who promised
is reliable
and trustworthy
and faithful.

Hebrews 10:23 AMP

May our **Lord Jesus Christ** himself and **God** our **Father,**
who loved us
and through grace
gave us eternal comfort
and good **hope,**
comfort your hearts
and strengthen them
in every good work
and word.

2 Thessalonians 2:16–17 NRSV

God, who began
the good work
within you,
will continue
his work
until it is
finally finished
on the day
when **Christ Jesus**
returns.

Philippians 1:6 NLT

We look forward with **hope** to that wonderful day when the glory of our great **God** and **Savior, Jesus Christ,** will be revealed.

Titus 2:13 NLT

May the **God**
of **hope**
fill you
with all joy
and peace
as you trust in **him,**
so that you may
overflow with **hope**
by the power
of the **Holy Spirit.**

Romans 15:13 NIV